RYSE

RYSE

Regain Your Self-Esteem

Brahim Derder

Writers Club Press
San Jose New York Lincoln Shanghai

RYSE
Regain Your Self-Esteem

Writers Club Press
an imprint of iUniverse.com, Inc.

For information address:
iUniverse.com, Inc.
5220 S 16th, Ste. 200
Lincoln, NE 68512
www.iuniverse.com

ISBN: 0-595-17125-7

Printed in the United States of America

I dedicate this book to my mother. As a child, I had lots of friends, some of whom tried to put me down at times. My mother always told them, "my son will be somebody someday". That uplifting message stayed with me along the highs and lows of life. Even my father at times, perhaps unintentionally, also disparaged and belittled me, and my mother came to my rescue, telling my father, you guessed it, "my son will be somebody someday".

Brahim Derder
12/17/2000

CONTENTS

I would like to thank Marie Stark, for her assistance in typing this book and all her unceasing moral support.

I also wish to thank my son Omar, who despite his young age, understood the value of giving encouraging messages, and the value of self-esteem.

INTRODUCTION

What is the difference between being alive or dead? What is the difference between living life to the fullest (happy, successful, as one wants his or her life to be) and living life just by surviving (seeing life as a burden)? What is the difference between successful people and failures, between sharp, assertive, successful people and timid, withdrawn people?

Human beings range from the very insecure, shy, completely withdrawn, just barely surviving to the secure, self-confident, living-lover, assertive, successful. In other words, humans span the spectrum of life just like other life-like phenomena (sound spectrum, light spectrum, etc.).

If we draw a line to represent the life spectrum it would look like Figure 1.

Figure 1

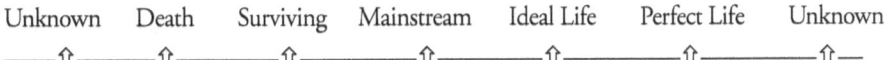

| Unknown | Death | Surviving | Mainstream | Ideal Life | Perfect Life | Unknown |

The majority of people live within the mainstream range and this includes people with medium self-esteem and image. Then, there is a good percentage of the people who are self-trapped in the surviving range mode. We say self-trapped because the majority of these people have been driven to the surviving zone (range) by outside forces (parents, all others, etc.). They did not do anything to reject it, thereby they accepted the trap and it became basically self-imposed since they did not do anything to get out of the surviving zone. For example, a person who stays in an abusive marriage or an employee who holds on to a dead-end job because of the fear of venturing into new zones of life (a new marriage, a new job) is a typical person who self-imposes a trap to stay where he/she is. How to get out of a surviving zone into a mainstream zone? Firstly, all of us have developed our personality with its web of traits from childhood and our growing circumstances. Consequently, we view the world through the perceptions we developed and not through reality. We interpret all events through our preconceived perceptions. For example, two people might react to frustration and anger in opposite ways.

How we were raised makes up the bulk of what drives or motivates us today. Again, reality and our own interpretation of it sometimes are completely different and that's where the problem lies. We filter our perceptions of events through our own eyes and that is not reality. In essence, we developed a complete set of values about ourselves and the outside world based on our own experiences which might have nothing to do with reality (cause and effect). For example, there is a story about a woman in the old days whose house got burned to the ground. She escaped and when the house collapsed and burned she returned and found a lamb well cooked—the lamb did not escape. This happened before man discovered cooking. The woman started moving things and in the process, she got her fingers stuck in the juicy lamb and she wiped the juice on her lips. The juice tasted really good. The woman decided to taste a piece of the lamb and it tasted good. She ate and enjoyed herself. From then on whenever she wanted to cook a lamb she burned her house down with a lamb chained inside. The moral of the story is that reality and our interpretation of it are different just like this woman who interpreted that burning the house is what causes the lamb to be cooked.

The reality as we know it is that the fire cooks the lamb. Reprogramming and healing our perception is the right way to deal with the world in a realistic way. We can change how we see and perceive our selves in a positive way; thereby we can regain our self-esteem simply by believing in our selves as capable as any body else.

CHILDHOOD

Problem Definition and how or why a person loses her or his self-esteem?

CAUSES OF SELF-ESTEEM LOSS:

There are many causes of losing one's self-esteem: Here are the main causes:

Childhood

Parents instill in one self-defeating beliefs and values; by putting him or her down and discouraging her or him from taking risks in the name of love. Children believe their parents and see them as role models.

School

Usually teachers, classmates, and test grades have influence on one's self-esteem. Put-downs, for example, by teachers or classmates have a negative effect on one's self-esteem. Religious conditioning of one's unworthiness contributes to one's low self-esteem as well.

ADULTHOOD

This period in one's life starts when one gets married, gets a job, or simply when one starts interacting with adults. In this stage adults affect one's self-esteem in many ways. For example, in a dysfunctional marriage where domestic violence is the norm, one spouse usually abuses the other verbally, using put-downs or even physically. In reciprocation the other spouse tries to fight back by using, usually, the same behavior—put-downs (true or false), or physical. Such a marriage ends, usually, either in divorce if not treated with proper therapy and both spouses are willing to compromise and change the addictive low self-esteem behavior, or in a perpetual addictive poisonous cruel treatment of each other that ultimately ends in a disaster (murder, etc.). And unfortunately the kids grow up in a dysfunctional environment.

Also, adults can receive negative influence to their self-esteem from coworkers on the job or from any other adult they come in contact with. Close friends or friends in general influence one's self-esteem positively or negatively in a very strong way. Therefore, friends must be selected carefully. Being exposed to negative self-esteem (as children or adults) causes us to learn distorted beliefs about ourselves and others. These distorted beliefs lead one to behave in self-defeating ways. All these negative self-esteem influences causes one to harbor deep feelings that something is wrong with him or her. Self-acceptance becomes a problem, because one believes or at least perceives herself or himself as abnormal (something is wrong with me because of all these negative influences from childhood to adulthood).

CONSEQUENCES OF LOW SELF-ESTEEM

Results of one's low self-esteem are devastating if not corrected. Most of the time, low self-esteem results in a miserable marriage (ultimately a dysfunctional family with dysfunctional kids) or a failure on the job or in business, or failure in any endeavor one undertakes. In addition to individual failures and unhappy lives, society suffers as well—most criminals, thieves, nonproductive members of society have low self-esteem and society ends up paying for them.

SYMPTOMS OF LOW SELF-ESTEEM

Persons with low self-esteem exhibit specific behavior and attitudes. Some of the important ones are:

1. They punish themselves severely when they make a mistake because they think they are the mistake. Their typical statements are: "should have", "must", etc.

2. Resistance to change: they try hard to keep the status quo (as it is); they do not venture into the unfamiliar and cling to the usual (things and routines they know).

3. Reacting rather than initiating actions. They tend to spend most of their time getting upset and angry at problems and worries instead of trying to solve them.

4. They feel victimized. They tend not to take responsibility but blame life (the spouse, the boss, anybody else) for their predicaments.

5. They hold on to resentment. They hold on to old hurts and painful memories, they are stuck in the past and vow not to forgive themselves or others for the wrongs already done and gone in the past. This holds negative energy inside them which can be converted to useful positive energy such as self-acceptance, self-forgiving, making friend with so called "old enemies", and living a normal happy life.

6. They want what they cannot have. This is exhibited usually when they devalue what they possess and wish for things they cannot have. As the old adage says, the grass is always greener on the other side.

7. They are pessimistic: most of the time they expect the worst out of life. And the self-fulfilling prophecy becomes reality for them. Some individuals even wish to die to escape their self-made painful reality.

8. Fear dominates their lives: low self-esteem individuals believe that life is always serious and must be taken as such always, in other words fun is a waste of time and is not necessary. They tend to live a life of surviving not enjoying life.

9. They always worry about "what if" instead of "what is". They subscribe to catastrophic thinking which causes them a great deal of worry, anxiety, and unnecessary mental crisis. For example if one's spouse is late, he or she starts to worry about the worst that can happen, such as cheating, accident, etc.

10. They feel unworthy. They put up a false front. They think if they are themselves others will not accept them even though in reality they are like everyone else.

11. They are perpetual people pleasers. They think gaining other people's approval is a prerequisite for their happiness and success.

12. They neglect themselves. Usually they attend to others' needs and neglect their own essential needs because of their low self-image.

13. They look outside themselves for happiness. This is demonstrated when they engage in unsafe sex, overeating, taking drugs, gambling, working compulsively, drinking, etc. These things, they think, keep their minds off their problems.

14. They think moving to a new place will leave behind all their problems. They tend to believe anywhere is better than where they live. Again the misconception of "the grass is greener on the other side" takes charge in their lives. This is wrong because wherever one moves to, he takes his character and all the above beliefs, and things do not change within.

We can rediscover the world we live in and start enjoying instead of taking it for granted. Life is not a monotony, it is a thrill. Think of three or more things you like to do that make you happy. Write them down, and just do them, you'll see that you can choose to enjoy life again.

PESSIMISM

Again our childhood has a lot to do with what we see and how we see things today as adults. Statements such as the following:

1. Life is full of problems.

2. Always assume people are bad.

3. I cannot handle most challenges I meet.

4. I am a loser.

5. I do not like the way I look.

6. I am not a worthy person...etc.

As adults many of us continue thinking addictively. Our addictive thinking tells us nothing we ever do is good enough. This habit of selecting the negative over the positive eventually leads us to believe that everything is negative. We look at the dark side of life rather than the bright one. Few of us attain the skill of optimism. Most of us, rather, carry a magnifying glass looking for flaws and defeats. We are critical of others and berate ourselves. We wage a war on ourselves and see an enemy in others. We moan and groan about our misery and blame someone else for our despair and unhappiness. Addictive thinkers lower morale in the house, on the job, and in social gatherings they can be divisive because they dump their addictive waste on everyone else. We, unconsciously, distance ourselves from the addictive persons. This is how negative reality is created.

Self-sabotage occurs when we set our standards so high that we are bound to fail. We set ourselves up to failure by comparing ourselves to the best of everything in every category.

OPTIMISM

The skill of optimism says: make peace with yourself; you no longer need addictive thoughts because they do not fit your healing process in life. Optimism teaches us that life, like a coin, has two sides. Developing this skill leads us to dwell on happiness rather than despair, or at least allocate equal time to solving problems and an equal time to just enjoying life. This means ignoring problems won't make them disappear but we can decide to give happiness an equal time. Both sorrow and happiness are part of life. The dualities of joy and sadness, hate and love, right and wrong, good and evil—all are part of life's total package. As a discovery of yourself, list three positive traits and three negative traits of yourself.

POSITIVE VS. NEGATIVE MESSAGES

Healing yourself and regaining your self-esteem begins with self-acceptance and this means releasing/erasing other people's opinions (the negative ones). To do this and any other task requires practice/action. The following is an example of what we must erase:

Negative Message	*Healing Message*
1. I want to be loved by everyone.	It would be nice to be loved by everyone, but that is impossible.
2. Others upset me.	I choose to let others upset me.
3. Life is full of pain and misery.	Life is full of happiness and what I choose it to be.
4. Things have to be perfect for me to be happy.	Life is uncertain and people, myself included, are not perfect.

Keep in mind that happiness is not having what we want but wanting what we have already. When we think of happiness in terms of what we want, we already are operating from a status of *lack* and negativity. We are focusing on what is missing in our lives, and we are trying to convince ourselves that something or someone else will fill our void and make us whole and happy.

EXPECTATION

Thinking the worst brings the worst into our lives. Our thoughts and expectations create our realities in life because expectations affect the way we behave and the way we behave affects how others respond to us. This is also known as self-fulfilling prophecy (we get what we expect). Everything that happens is a thought before it is an action. Expecting problems and unhappiness brings exactly that.

Fear of failure is a negative motivator. At the deepest core of our feeling of fear of failure, within, we believe we are failures, no matter how successful we are in the outer world.

You Can Handle Anything

To combat this self-defeating feeling, it is eventually easy to simply accept ourselves no matter what happened because "we can handle anything", believing that we can live with any outcome. Besides, life itself is limited so why worry so much as if we are here on this earth forever—when we accept the fact that we can handle anything that happens to us, including death itself, we become happy.

We must see failure as an opportunity. We can learn from our mistakes and failures and correct our thinking/action accordingly. We should always expect the best life has to offer.

CREATING A HEALTHY SELF-IMAGE

The good news is that we can create whatever we want in life simply by expecting it and believing it—of course we must act, not just think and wish. For example, if you want to create a healthy friendship with someone:

1. First, get rid of any self-defeating thoughts that you are undeserving or unlikable or inadequate. You begin to think of yourself as worthy and likable based on your positive personality strengths.

2. Behave in accordance with these expectations.

3. Your self-confidence and positive image attract people to you.

4. If you are persistent and consistent with your expectations, over time people will be drawn and attracted to you.

5. Ultimately you will find friends you enjoy being with.

Just because we had a painful past doesn't mean we must continue living a painful life forever. We can create the kind of life we want by changing our outlook on the future and erasing the past and believing that we were not responsible for what has happened. We did the best *we knew in the past* and we suffered for it—we paid for it—and therefore we can start a new happy life now.

YOU ARE ATTRACTED TO PEOPLE LIKE YOU

We tend to attract persons into our lives who think, feel, and behave like us—and this is because we like to stay with what we know and do not wish to venture into the new and unknown. It is the opposite of the physics principle of magnetism (opposites attract). In human life similar and like attract similars. It has been stated that thoughts and feelings have their own magnetic energy that attracts energy of a similar nature. This energy has its frequency and unique characteristics.

This theory is clearly manifested in the types of relationships children from dysfunctional homes form in adulthood. Most of these adults tend to marry and become friends with adults from dysfunctional homes. Also observe that people who dislike themselves, or who are confused tend to gravitate around similar persons. We can rescue ourselves by removing ourselves from addictive relationships (friendships, marriage, etc.) and seek people who enhance our self-worth.

BECOMING INDEPENDENT

As we begin to heal our self-esteem, for example removing ourselves from codependent relationships, we rock the boat and we begin to assert ourselves and to set boundaries. Speaking up breaks the addictive pattern and friends, loved ones may be surprised because they are used to us being codependent. But we must continue taking care of ourselves even when others try to make us feel guilty by showing discomfort or whatever way of guilt they use to stop us from regaining our self-esteem. We must establish boundaries because everybody needs boundaries to grow. Boundaries tell us how far we can go. Boundaries allow us to keep our individuality by remaining separate human beings. Boundaries let others know how far they can come and go. Boundaries define how far we can go; barricades prevent us from going anywhere. Thus boundaries are different from barricades.

Detachment is one good way to establish boundaries. Sometimes the negativity of coworkers, family members, or friends pulls us down. We can detach ourselves while maintaining our love for them. Detachment might mean physically removing ourselves temporarily from a situation. *We do not have to take on the problems and negativity of anyone.*

As we start to regain our self-esteem by getting healthier, our relationships start changing too. We find it impossible to stay in relationships that continue to be addictive. Always remember others always resist change because they feel threatened. Ultimately, we will support, forgive and care for ourselves, and enjoy our own company and become our own best friend.

What Goes Around Comes Around

Whatever thoughts we put out come back to us in some form, similar to a boomerang. For example, sending out positive thoughts, feelings, and actions causes positive experiences to come back to us. Metaphysics states that we all belong to *one* big energy source. We are one great mass of sub-atomic molecules, each within our own electromagnetic energy field. Even in modern physics the concept of oneness has credibility. Physics claims that when atoms within a molecule align in certain ways, the rest of the atoms follow in the same order. It is the same with people. When the majority agrees about an issue the rest follows.

Because of the oneness concept, when we help someone we help our-selves. When we love ourselves, we transfer that love (self-love) to others in some form.

Our unhappiness comes from addictive thinking. No one else is to blame for our mental mindset. Negatively reacting to someone else, who is different from us, boomerangs back to us.

Research established that negative thoughts always create negative emotions, and negative emotions lead to the release of biochemical engines in the body that creates side effects. Our anger can kill us and laughter can heal us. Anger causes the release of the hormone epinephrine which makes our hearts beat faster and thus blood pressure rises.

Research links workaholism to the release of adrenaline in the body. Adrenaline is a hormone produced by the body under stress. Adrenaline has an effect similar to the effect of amphetamines or speed. And this is why, some psychologists believe, workaholics subject themselves and their surroundings to high stress so that they can get high. They become addicted to workaholism because it provides them with the fix (adrenaline). Holding on to anger and resentment has a boomerang effect. It hurts us more than it hurts the others. Turning anger into love boomerangs back to us and allows us to heal and regain our self-esteem.

ADAPT TO NEW THINGS AND EVENTS

Our lives work well when we fit our thoughts, feelings, and actions into our environment instead of trying to fit our environment into our thoughts, feelings, and actions. Knowing and acknowledging that there is a power greater than ourselves help us turn problems over to that power and relieves us of worrying—remember the universe functioned from the beginning of time without us.

We get frustrated in traffic jams, we become angry with people who have different beliefs from us.... we waste a lot of energy getting mad at our daily conditions, instead of accepting them and living our lives within their boundaries.

The serenity prayer says, "God, grant me the wisdom to accept the things I cannot change, courage to change the things I can, and wisdom to know the difference".

WE CREATE DISHARMONY FOR OURSELVES IN THREE WAYS

Forcing—we try to impose and control others and situations.

Resisting—we deny accepting the world as it is and put up resistance.

Holding—we cling to the familiar and avoid change or the unknown in favor of habit and routine.

FORCING

We can only control a few things, therefore we can be happy by accepting the world as it is—the world is already in order and does not need to be put in order, we simply need to put ourselves in unison with this existing order. For example, many things do not warrant fighting for, because we waste valuable energy when fighting for something unworthy or that we can't change—some things cannot be changed no matter what. We are not and cannot always be right and the others wrong.

It is not our responsibility to fix the other persons even if they are wrong.

The need for control and forcing our way comes from fear of something negative. We cannot change our spouses or parents or anyone else to our way no matter how hard we try. We can only accept them as they are and change our REACTIONS to them. Serenity and happiness come from accepting people and things as they are.

RESISTING

Look at palm trees, they survive the strongest storms because they are flexible enough to bend, swing, and move with the wind, not against the forces of the wind. We loosen ourselves by becoming flexible, spontaneous, and willing to bend. Resistance in our daily lives stalls the process of healing and regaining our self-esteem.

There is a difference between persistence and stubbornness. We are persistent when we know we are right and try *new* ways when blocked but we are stubborn when we know we are wrong and cannot admit or when clinging to one known way or thing rather than exploring new ways.

CLINGING

Everything in nature is constantly changing, therefore we must be changing accordingly—we are a part of this changing world. Usually we resist change whether the change is sought or imposed or happens by design or change and sadly we cling to old habits.

Safety aside, we heal when we walk into and face our fears; we can win and conquer fear only when we face it.

Giving up forcing, resisting, and clinging leads us to taking responsibility for our personal healing.

Do Not Carry Others Guilt

Events of life are always changing. Being able to adapt to these changes is the key to resolving them. For example, people who are feeling guilty always try to project their guilt onto others. They feel bad because of their actions and to protect themselves they try to make others responsible for their actions. They are always on the defensive and they try to tell everybody they are right (righteous) and all their problems are caused by others. It is a self-defense mechanism. They use it to shield themselves from feeling bad by blaming others for all their problems.

Do not fall into the traps of these people. Make a commitment to yourself not to accept their guilt. You know that they are guilty of what they are trying to charge you with. Say to yourself: I am not going to feel guilty because I did my best and they are guilty.

Dealing with Change

Very few things in this life do not change, if any at all. Things are changing as we speak, as they say. The cycle of change is everywhere and that makes life dynamic and interesting. Knowing how to deal with change is the key to happiness and to a good living.

First of all, there are a few principles we must be aware of. We must believe that change is good because it brings new things to us. Change is like a challenge and if we accept it as a good thing for us, then we deal with it with a positive attitude and the chances are very high that we will get good results from any change. Change is always good for us no matter how we perceive the change. Change is a natural process, and a by-product of being alive.

Some people are complacent with a simple life that has little change and those are usually the ones who dread change and are terrified of it. Change can bring their self-esteem into question, and doubt because they do not accept change as a fact of life. They sometimes break into pieces for they think they cannot deal with change and they will lose to change something. The things they fear to lose are in their heads and not real usually. Consequently, they start worrying and begin to second-guess their self-esteem values. They compare themselves to other people who deal with change in a positive way. Here lies the problem with change rejecters or simple-life acceptors or simply let us call them the non-adventurers. For example, they hate any little change, they like to stay in the same position and reject any opportunities of promotions for the fear of having to deal with change. The non-adventurers like to stay in a dysfunctional marriage because of the fear of dealing with a new life, a new spouse for example, or simply the thought of being alone devastates them. Then, there are people who are on the move and love to engage in new endeavors in pursuit of change. These are the people who are constantly looking for adventure and uncertainty does not scare them, but it excites them and motivates them to face new change and its challenges, let us call these the adventurers. These people love change and actually seek it when it does not come their way. Life to them is a good continuous spectrum of good change that brings them fortune and only good things. They welcome a promotion and seek it if it does not come in time. Their self-esteem is always intact and high and actually they use their positive attitude in dealing with change to build their self-esteem even more.

So, accept change as a good opportunity and an enjoyable adventure in your life and it will be and watch your self-esteem increase in its value. Your life becomes happier and worrying to the point of sickness disappears.

DEALING WITH SELF-ESTEEM BUSTERS

Handling unwanted events, actions, or simply call them unwanted "things" is usually done in one of two ways: 1) by using logical reasoning. Using this method to deal with things is the right way to use if it is used fairly and correctly. For example, a friend of mine told me that his wife always tried to destroy his self-esteem by putting him down. He finally faced her by telling her, "you are putting me down and disparaging me because you are jealous of me—I have more education than you for one, I know how to handle people and deal with them better than you; you are always getting in trouble with others and you do not have even a GED and I have a Masters Degree, people always tell you how successful and good I am. Therefore it is obvious that you are jealous of me." The husband, in this example, used reason to respond to his wife's invalidations and chances are that she was convinced that she was putting him down because she felt insecure, scared, that he might leave her for another woman. Most importantly, she might have stopped after she became aware of her actions and their motives.

Another simple example, a father tells his son, "You got a C in Math because you did not study enough, not because you are less than the students who got A's, you can get an A if you put in A effort into preparing".

The bad news in using logical reasoning is that only some people become convinced once a reasonable and logical explanation is presented to them and consequently the problem is resolved peacefully.

The problem with most people who believe and use logical reasoning is when they deal with irrational, unreasonable, incomprehensible things or people. Reasonable, logical people become frustrated, afraid, confused, and depressed when dealing with unreasonable things or people. Because there are people who do not believe in logic and reason, these people, in all probability, have been deceived and abused by others who used false and unfair reasoning, thereby these people became unreasonable themselves because they lost faith in reasoning things. This leads to a vicious repeated cycle because these people will pass on the same method of loss of faith to others they deal with.

As you can conclude, reasoning does not work with all people. In the real world it rarely works by itself alone because you must keep in mind and be convinced that you are dealing with an imperfect world. This is a world that has good and bad in the same person and people affect each other. If indeed logic, fairness, and reason alone can solve problems then there would be no world wars or any wars.

However, it is worth trying to use reason first, keeping in mind that you might have to use other means to resolve problems.

Try using the following first when handling self-esteem destroyers:

Diplomacy, professionalism, human respect, patience, empathy, but do not use insinuation, labeling, judgment, self-righteousness, generalization, in other words, in this stage use only REASONABLE MEANS.

If reason does not work, then use the second method:

2) Cause and effect: This is a method that relies on cause and an action fitting the cause. In this method you act and not reason. For example, a spouse who abused the other and reasoning did not work, separation (action) might bring the other spouse to reason.

JUST DO IT NOW

Just Do It Now

Doing something is the key at this stage. It is time for action; actions speak louder than words. Scream loudly at self-esteem destroyers. In reality there is no one response to an invalidator, but here are some examples:

A) Ask the invalidator to REPEAT what he /she said. This usually makes him or her paraphrase the insult in a better way.

B) Facing and confronting the invalidator. Sometimes just keeping eye contact with them and non-verbally letting them know that you know what they are up to will stop them from going further.

Problem Solving Method

Problems arising from different causes, including invalidators and others, can be contained and controlled. If problems are not resolved or at least controlled, they become like a brush fire, destroying and burning everyone involved. Therefore, problems must be swiftly resolved or at least put under control. There is no one formula to resolve all problems, however, there are methods to bring basically any problem under control. One of the methods that has been tested and proven to work includes some logical steps.

Assume the following problems, for example, your ex-spouse is very vindictive and she is trying to use every method and trick in the book to harass you and possibly destroy you consciously or unconsciously.

I) The first step, *problem definition*, can be as follows. Ex spouse is using all possible actions and dirty tricks, illegal actions, false allegations against me, defamation of character, etc. In summary, ex spouse is trying to destroy my self-esteem.

II) The second step, *possible outcomes* can be: 1) people will believe her attacks against me and that might affect me negatively by alienating my friends from me and creating possible enemies. 2) Courts might believe her allegations and hurt me financially and psychologically. 3) I might after her repeated false allegations doubt myself and start letting my self-esteem be affected. If she succeeds in affecting my self-esteem negatively, of course with my permission, I suffer the consequences. 4) She tries to turn my kids against me. There might be more possible outcomes. List all you can list now, then go back later and list whatever comes to your mind. Sit with a friend or a professional counselor and list possible outcomes. Once you know the possible effects or outcomes of the problem, you break it down to even smaller pieces to become more manageable. From the above possible outcomes/effects select the third step:

III) The third step is: *accept the worst possible outcome.* Once you accept the worst possible outcome—I say possible because it might never happen, it has been established that the worst possible things we worry about never happen, you free yourself from worrying and validate your inner powers. In other words, once you accept the worst outcome as indeed a possibility you have practically said to yourself: I can handle this. Once you convince yourself that you can handle the worst, worry disappears and your self-esteem is shielded from any damage because the problem becomes manageable like any simple project.

IV) The fourth and last step is:

Improve on the worst outcome: By analyzing and breaking the problem to its smallest components and narrowing it down to its worst outcome you have empowered yourself to deal with the problem without pressure and in a logical manner; you have separated the problem from your emotions and self-esteem. Now, you can, in all probability, find some logical solutions.

This method can be memorized as *People Define Possible Outcomes, Accept Worst Outcome, Improve on Worst Outcome.*

METHODS INVALIDATORS USE TO DESTROY YOUR SELF-ESTEEM

Projection: Projection is a psychological method invalidators use to manipulate others. Basically, the invalidator takes his own feelings and puts their responsibility for them onto another person—projects his feelings onto another person. For example, an individual who hates you says, "I think you hate me". This statement makes you question yourself and shifts your attention from the other person to yourself. Generally, when people accuse others of things, they themselves are guilty of their own accusations, but they attempt to project them onto others to make themselves feel good.

Uncertainty: Invalidators try to keep you in a constant state of uncertainty so they can keep you in suspense. For example, an invalidator suddenly becomes hostile and the next moment he becomes loving and caring. His strategy is to keep you off balance and ultimately under his control. Your self-esteem is at his mercy and he tries to destroy it any time he finds an opportunity.

Generalization: Self-esteem busters use this tactic quite often, because any simple event practically leads the invalidator to seize the chance and exaggerate by generalizing. For example, a woman who did not get what she wanted from her husband would say to him "you are not a man like all other men, you are less of a man". Obviously, she is exaggerating and not even addressing the real problem but attacking her husband instead. Generalization can affect one's self esteem very negatively.

How to Recognize Invalidation

It has been discovered through simple observations and systematic research that self-esteem and or self-confidence loss can be caused in childhood or adulthood.

We see, in our modern society, people who are at their ultimate top of self-confidence, and /or self-esteem, in business, social life, and all other aspects of life. Suddenly, because of some event such as divorce, simple disagreements or other mischiefs we see the same people start to lose their self-confidence and their success in business, social life, and practically in all endeavors of life begin to decline. We know that nothing happens without a cause; there is always a cause and effect.

YOU ARE BEING INVALIDATED DEVIOUSLY

First, what is invalidation? Invalidation in simple layman's terms is putting other people down, discrediting other's achievements and trying to destroy their self-esteem for the purpose of controlling them or simply to satisfy some gratification by proving to themselves (the invalidators) that they can destroy others' self-esteem, and make themselves look bigger.

Be very careful when a disagreement arises between you and someone else. Whenever there is a conflict, be it a simple or a complex conflict, between you and others, an invalidator is on your trail. An invalidator can be your own spouse, parent, lover, sister, brother, coworker, partner, or anybody for that matter.

The rule to *identify* your invalidator is simple. First, something happens as the cause of what will lead to a chain of events. This causes (the cause) the invalidator to start, consciously, or unconsciously, his or her invalidation attacks. Fortunately for you after reading this book, you will be able to recognize the symptoms of the invalidation immediately.

Self-Confidence

Nobody is perfect and that is okay. However, there are some people who tend to feel depressed, down, inadequate, without any confidence in their abilities—even though in their past they proved to be capable of the same things they feel incapable of now. This feeling of sudden loss of one's self-confidence comes from the concept of expectation. We expect to always win, do well, and so do others. Others expect us or so we think, to always win and do well. Some people, because of this expectation of themselves resort to depression, self-pity so that others will not expect anything of them; since they think others will not expect anything of a depressed person. It is an excuse people use when they lose their confidence and become depressed and sometimes dysfunctional.

The reality of losing one's self esteem or confidence is simply an escape from facing the world as one should. It's okay to make mistakes, mistakes are part of living. To regain one's confidence, one must push ahead and try the tasks that create fear and not expect to always succeed. Self-confidence comes from trying, not avoiding even trying. In small steps, one can make progress. Just as the old adage says: a long journey starts with one step. So start today with a simple task you have been postponing and be satisfied with just trying and taking action, regardless of the outcome. This will start your confidence building.

JUDGMENT AS AN INVALIDATION

The easiest way, probably, for the invalidator is to use judgment when trying to destroy your self-esteem. For example, he/she might say "you are not a responsible person" no matter how much confidence you have, you will, probably, start to doubt yourself, especially if this statement is repeated frequently to you. Again, the invalidator attacks your self-esteem, not the problem.

VICTIMS OF LOW SELF-ESTEEM GET REWARDS

People with low self-esteem thrive on claiming to always be victims. They might blame others for being where they are or they might blame incidents and events. They try very hard to prove to the world that they are not responsible for their dilemma and try to gain sympathy by claiming helplessness and righteousness. Even when things start to go right for them, they try to find a way to mess it up so they can continue their victim status and get others to feel sorry for them. This is a reward for them when others come to their rescue or simply sympathize with them. They miss that if they are not victims.

The right thing to do, though, is that one must take full charge of his actions and realize that he or she can determine his or her worth and not others. One must free himself from the victim syndrome and that is by simply being responsible and stop blaming others for his or her problems, and moving full speed ahead without seeking others approval or sympathy. It is the only way to live free, and regain self-esteem and be happy.

THE CYCLE OF INVALIDATION

Invalidation is developed basically in early stages of childhood. Most likely from parents, teachers, brothers and sisters or anyone else close to us. An invalidator usually had been in his or her childhood abused and invalidated. A victim of invalidation has been subjected to repeated acts of invalidation until he or she became almost if not completely self-convinced that he or she is bad. Once this process occurs of being unconsciously convinced that he or she was bad and that they deserved all the abuses, mostly invalidation or self-esteem destruction, the damage become serious and his or her self-esteem gets damaged severely.

Later in their lives, victims of invalidation, when they come across anybody with a different opinion other than theirs, defend themselves even if they know they are wrong. They are always on the defensive because they unconsciously want to prove to the whole world that they are not wrong or bad. They fight everybody who does not agree with them because they subconsciously see the other person as an invalidator. They try to tell everybody how bad the other person is and how victimized they are. They believe that they are always right. They basically vow not to be invalidated again as they were in their childhood. This behavior leads them to the extreme where they become self-righteous and the truth becomes irrelevant to them. They, consequently, become invalidators themselves and the cycle repeats itself.

SELF-ESTEEM AND YOUR BELIEF SYSTEM

A belief system is a set of different rules one acquires, just like learning skills, mostly in his or her early age. A belief system includes religious convictions, social norms/rules that one believes in and is convinced of. There are other sources of one's belief system. Based on one's beliefs, his/her self-esteem depends almost linearly and directly. For example, if one has strong beliefs in God and all His associated unlimited powers, practically nothing bad will affect him. Also, if one has strong beliefs in his abilities and skills, usually others cannot affect his/her self-esteem seriously, because people with strong self-esteem/confidence in themselves have a strong shield already (their belief in themselves).

Social support systems have a significant influence on one's self-esteem as well. Having a good supportive social individual/group will cancel the negative attacks on your self-esteem. This happens when indeed your support system understands the attacks and replenishes your self-esteem with positive statements/actions.

HEALING YOUR SELF-ESTEEM

We can heal our self-esteem if we indeed believe that we have the power to make the change from low self-esteem to a healthy normal self-esteem. Our thoughts can be governed by new beliefs. We can change ourselves by changing our thoughts. There are some major aspects in our personality that we must address and make some changes in order for us to ultimately *regain our self-esteem*. The following are the major building blocks that must be analyzed and redressed.

PERCEPTION

Our perceptions are developed early on in our childhood. The perceptions we are exposed to in childhood impact our outlooks in our adulthood. For example, having been raised in a dysfunctional family leads us to learn a series of distorted beliefs about ourselves and others. These distorted beliefs interfere with our feelings and behavior when interacting with the real world. We usually do not act in self-enhancing ways. For example, because of our negative upbringing we tend to think *when we make a mistake that we are the mistake.* We do not separate the mistakes we make from what we are. *A person with a normal self-esteem acknowledges his or her mistake and simply corrects it,* but a low self-esteem individual believes, when he or she makes a mistake, that he or she is the mistake and keeps dwelling on it and punishes himself or herself severely. This is an addictive type of thinking always results in an unhappy life. As children, we developed functional feelings or dependent feelings about ourselves such as confident, attractive, ugly, shameful, smart, stupid, intelligent, etc. These feelings depend on the background we grew up in. We can start to look at ourselves objectively, we can realize that we are not the problem but we are like everyone else. The only difference between us and them is our perception of ourselves. *Healing and regaining self-esteem is a process we can enjoy doing.* First of all, we can see ourselves as we truly are (healthy), we can erase the distorted beliefs in our background and replace these erroneous beliefs with the normal ones—that we are not different from others. Loving ourselves unconditionally, no matter what our problems, and forgiving ourselves for making mistakes permits us to remove abnormal feelings and start a happy life. In essence, we re-engineer our childhood by giving ourselves the love and nurturing we missed in our childhood.

Loving oneself is not selfish. *On the contrary, how can one love others if he or she does not even love himself or herself.* So, love and treat yourself as number one always.

SELF-POWER

We are in charge of our lives and we must believe that we are empowered, *because we are unless we relinquish our power to someone else or become addicted to drugs that will control our lives.* When we believe that we have power over our thoughts, feelings, and actions we indeed control our lives the way we want. Individuals without control of their lives say things like "there is nothing I can do", "she or he made me feel like nothing", "if it were not for him or her I would not be in this predicament or mess". This is a typical addictive thinking developed from early childhood usually.

Dysfunctional families produce children with control as a big issue for them because they, the children, have witnessed parents struggling for control. They blame others and situations for all their problems. These children, and now adults, develop learned helplessness—that no matter what they do their fate is out of their control. Some people call them externalizers because they believe external powers and forces control their lives.

All of us are powerless, but not helpless. Regaining our self-energy must include the belief that a search for total power is not a mirage, but it can be achieved, and become reality.

There are things we have control over, but there are other things that we have no control over no matter how hard we try. We are powerless over the external world, such as the weather, *other people's conduct,* but we have inner power to heal ourselves because we have control over ourselves and how we think and act. *Helplessness occurs when we give up our courage to change the things in our lives that we can control and change.* We should not give our personal power to writers, spouses, therapists, gurus or lovers to exercise control over us. Again, relinquishing our power to another person makes us helpless, codependent, and victims of life. Peace and serenity come from accepting our powerlessness over these things we cannot change, courage to change things we can and the wisdom to know the difference between what we can change and what we cannot change.

Defining and determining the things *we can change* is the first critical step in healing our self-esteem. Our energy is limited and wasting it on trying to change the things that are beyond our control or simply not changeable is a drain of our precious and limited energy. For example, trying to change a spouse who is a drug addict *or simply trying to change a spouse is a drain to our energy and always results in an unhappy life and miserable relationships.* Admitting our powerlessness over the past equips us with power to *respond to the future.*

We must believe that we have power to create our thoughts because this belief gives us power over circumstances and we stop making ourselves victims of circumstances. The difference between an empowered person and a victim of life is that the empowered person *learns life's lessons* whereas the victim *endures life's pain.* Empowerment means taking conscious responsibility for our life, instead of blaming others for our problems. Empowerment means turning obstacles into opportunities. *Empowerment means when we are down we know it is our mental attitude that needs changing not the world.*

Healthy Self-Esteem is Happiness

Achieving happiness and regaining our self-esteem depend on us and nobody else. Regaining our healthy self-esteem requires us to go through a joyful thought reconstruction process. We redirect our thinking, for example, from focusing on hardships and start looking for the possibilities and opportunities. We start looking into a new looking glass that reflects joy, beauty, truth, hope, and new possibilities for us; this leads to a healthy self-esteem and that results in our happiness.

Taking actions and making conscious decisions for ourselves play a big part in regaining and reclaiming our power in our lives and our self-esteem. *Any action is better than none.*

Our Inner Power

Regaining our self-esteem is within our inner self-control, not the outside world (wife, friends, girlfriend, etc.). Some of us who feel unfinished and incomplete often look outside ourselves to fill the void and feel happy. We get involved in unhealthy relationships, seek material possessions, and generally seek outside things. We look in the wrong places when we search outside ourselves for solutions to our life problems. As someone said, we are often so busy "getting there", that we forget we are already there and there is nowhere else to go. The treasure is within us, so only by our inner transformation do we make a significant change in improving our life and its quality. The inner connection is a perpetual pleasant journey. We never stop healing ourselves. We must learn to diminish our wants for material possessions—and this is very hard in a capitalistic system. In healing and regaining our self-esteem we must learn that the only way to attempt to change someone else is to change ourselves first and be a role model. *Regaining our self-esteem leads us to realize that we cannot control anyone or anything but ourselves and we are responsible, consequently, for ourselves only.* You are like the man riding his donkey. When he comes down from riding it he looks for his donkey and once he is on the ground he finds his donkey, but when he rides his donkey he thinks that his donkey has disappeared, when actually *he is* on top of his donkey! The donkey never disappeared, it's the man's perception.

If you want to change your life, you must change the way you think about yourself first. Looking in our inner selves allows us to see ourselves honestly and requires us to:

Acknowledge *all* the positive things about ourselves.

Love ourselves with no strings attached.

Forgive ourselves for our mistakes and go on with our lives.

We can correct our old patterns of behavior and thinking in the process of regaining our self-esteem by realizing:

Your addictive thinking came from addictive perceptions which we developed in our childhood through the caregivers (parents, brothers, sisters, neighbors, teachers, etc.)

That our life is where it is today because of our continued addictive thinking and there is only one way to change that—through continued change in our way of thinking and acting.

That abandoning our addictive way of thinking results in healthier ways of thinking, acting, feeling, etc.

That you must keep practicing all the concepts (optimism, positive expectation, self-control, etc.)

That a commitment must be adhered to no matter what happened, because through persistence we accomplish the goals we have set.

CONTROL YOUR THINKING
AND YOU CAN GET ANYTHING

Also, we must realize that because of our addictive thinking (withdrawal, irritability, complaining, and any negative thoughts) even our closest friends and family become annoyed.

Stay in control of the process of regaining your self-esteem because even in the process, somewhere along the line, the voice of addictive thinking still tries to hold conversation with us, especially before an event that might produce slight anxiety. Always intercept the negative and self-defeating thought, feelings and behavior by reminding yourself that you are in control of what you control and change and are not responsible for what you are not in control of (since you cannot change it).

Resolving to resolve our problems is the only way to ensure that we indeed permanently solve the problem and leave it behind us forever and move on with our lives.

Enjoy Life, not Endure it

Going within and facing our hurt and pain is the only way we will ever heal and regain our self-esteem. *As long as we flee from our inner feelings, we can never resolve them.* Living as a whole person is your right, regardless of your religious beliefs or their absence. This life is meant to be enjoyed and not endured. From the beginning of time, religions have tried to assist man in various establishments (mosques, churches, synagogues, etc.) and in our modern life psychologists try to help us, basically, in the same way. Psychology and all the studies of the human psyche try to help man cope and change through therapy and an entire gamut of methods. *Nothing will work unless the individual makes the effort,* consciously, continually, and with no retreat. Because trying anything, regaining your self-esteem, for example, requires conscious and continuous enjoyable work. *And what is more enjoyable than your success in life and good feelings about yourself?* Love yourself and use some positive statements you might keep reminding yourself of as you start your enjoyable journey or regaining your self-esteem.

Start Seeing Life Positively

Today, I am at peace with myself because I do not expect it from outside me (from a spouse, a friend, making more money, or any other source, even though these are okay but not essential.)

Problems I face daily are lessons, without them I do not learn new things.

I am on this earth for a short time, it is similar to a visit, therefore, I must enjoy it as a visit, knowing that it will end eventually.

I challenge you to be yourself, to pamper yourself, love yourself, forgive and care for yourself, and you will regain your self-esteem and live a happy life.

Vacuum of Erasing Old Ways

Getting rid of addictive thoughts, feelings, and behavior clears our mind for receiving healing, regaining our self-esteem, and being happy again. Harboring negative thoughts, feelings, and engaging in self-defeating actions leaves no free space for positive thoughts, feelings, and actions. This means that we must make room for the positive by letting go of the negative. Thinking positive or at least non-hostile thoughts about others, especially spouses, friends, enemies, etc. saves our mental energy and channels it toward future positive use. Admitting to ourselves that we cannot control everything that happens to us, but we are in charge of how we think, feel, and act under each circumstance. For example, if you receive some negative thought inputs from some friends, decide and act to remove this input by letting go of these unhealthy relationships to make room for healthy people to enter your life. Life teaches us to possess not give, not only with material things but with feelings as well—if we get something we win, but if we give up something, we lose.

Harboring vengeance and hatred hurts only us. It eats away at us like a disease. It keeps our thoughts always focused on the negative and leaves no space for new feelings. Headaches, ulcers, palpitations, nausea and other symptoms result from our storage of negative energy (thoughts and feelings).

The concept of vacuum is about releasing all the negative thoughts, feelings that can do us harm—anger, animosities, fear, worry, jealousy, hurt, depression, etc. As long as we hold on to these negatives, we have no room for healing ourselves and repairing our self-esteem.

The following ways help us evacuate our addictive thoughts and feelings:

1.   Talking to a therapist or a good friend helps us start moving these negatives out of our minds. Support groups, such as 12 step programs, also help us talk out thoughts and feelings in a caring atmosphere.

2.   Writing our thoughts down or speaking them into a tape recorders gets the flow moving outwards and away from us.

3.   Using creative outlets, such as art, drama, music, and poetry can help us express and release unhealthy feelings.

4.   Venting strong feelings of rage by pounding clay, batting a punching bag, or hitting our bed moves them out of our bodies onto other (inanimate) objects.

5.   Exercising in any form—running, aerobics, fast walking, etc. enables us to work out frustrations, angers, and other negative feelings.

6.   Using forgiveness is one valuable method of emptying our negative energy and creating a vacuum for positive energy flow. *Forgiving others for the wrongs they have committed against us is the ultimate act of self-love.* Forgiveness rids us of hurt and frees us to acquire positive feelings. Ironically, forgiving others benefits us, not the others. Silently let us forgive them regardless of whether they ever hear or accept our apology. Think of any person toward whom you harbor negative feelings and be ready to let the feelings go for your own sake. Say to yourself affirmations such as "Today I release all resentments that I carry. My heart refills with love and happiness. I will inventory my grudges and let them all go, and I refill with love. I bury the hatred and set myself free. I ask for strength to practice forgiveness while maintaining my sense of self worth and regaining my self-esteem."
Remember that you must forgive totally for the past, present, and future behaviors.

7.   *We have the choice:* We always have the choice over how we feel, think, and act, no matter how difficult things seem. We can never

erase the past and its mistakes, but we can choose our future. It takes effort and self-discipline, willingness to make choices, and openness to new ways. We heal our self-esteem by choosing the way we look at the world. Having filtered our lives up until now through the negative lenses of the past, we may need to train our eyes, ears, and all the other senses to look for the beauty, joy, fun, and happiness in life. When we live each day as if it's our first and last, our lives are happier. We must learn to act, not react. For example, many of us get angry easily with store clerks or anyone we find easy to dump our frustrations on. Some of us go through life reacting to life's random events. We respond in predictable ways without thinking about our choices.

We should think and then act. We make conscious choices that put us in charge of our lives.

The one thing no one can take away from us is the power of choice, no matter how hopeless our lives seem. Unfortunately, some of us choose to continue living in misery and continue complaining about the past. No matter how bad our yesterdays, we can choose to transform them into happy and fulfilling todays and tomorrows. However, we must choose to act and not sit down if we choose to get somewhere.

HEALING COMES FROM ACTION
AND NOT LETHARGY

Nothing ventured, nothing gained. Choose to stop using the old ways that do not work. Stop going back to the same people. If something is not working do something about it. We must try until we get it right. Unfortunately some of us limit ourselves—out of a need for security, for example. The more choices we have in life, the scarier it can be. Therefore, we eliminate choices by patronizing the same restaurant, holding the same job, following the same daily routine.

THOUGHTS FOR THE SOUL

1. Waiting for the perfect set of conditions is a wait forever. Nothing man-made can be absolutely perfect.

2. The test of a successful person is not an ability to eliminate all problems before they arise, but to meet and work out difficulties when they arise.

3. In any activity, cross bridges when you come to them, because you can't eliminate all risks.

4. Action feeds and strengthens confidence. Action cures fear and gains confidence. To fight fear, act. To increase fear, wait.

5. Ideas have value only when acted upon.

6. Don't waste time getting ready to act. Start acting now instead.

How to Get in the Mood for Work

1) Acting or even pretending to act precedes getting in the mood. I make myself sit down at my desk, then I pick up a pencil and go through mechanical motions of writing. I put down anything and sooner or later without my being conscious of it, my mind gets on the right track.

2) Most of the good ideas come from just getting to work.

3) Action precedes all—nothing starts itself.

4) Don't postpone getting started.

5) Mechanical action defeats fears. People who get things done in this world don't wait for the spirit to move them, they move the spirit.

6) People place confidence in the person who acts. They naturally assume he knows what he's doing.

GOAL SETTING

Changes in behavior precede changes in attitudes, meaning actions precede feelings such as smiling creates happiness, acting courageously leads to feelings of courage. In other words: actions cause and lead to feelings and attitudes.

1) Setting an objective will minimize your indecision in making choices about matters unrelated to your goal.

2) As you concentrate on your goals and ignore thoughts of failure, self-doubt, worry, anxiety, or less important matters, you will reach your objectives.

3) Without a goal, you will focus on your weaknesses and the possibilities of error and criticism.

4) Action will give you a sense of identity and will reduce conflict and inhibition.

5) Handle simple choices first, difficult ones last.

6) Focus on one objective at a time.

How to Think Big

1) Where success is concerned, people are not measured in inches, or pounds, or college degrees, or family background; they are measured by the size of their thinking.

2) To think big we must use words and phrases which produce big, positive mental images.

3) Big thinkers train themselves to see not just what is, but what can be.

4) It is not what one has that is important. Rather, it is how much one is planning to get that counts.

5) Practice adding value to things. Add value to house or computer to be sold. Look for ideas to make things worth more.

6) Visualize the best in a person.

7) Practice adding value to yourself.

8) Focus on the big picture, not the trivialities. It is much better to lose a battle and win the war than to win a battle and lose the war.

LIVE FREE OF FEAR

Fear can be broken down into three levels.

The First Level is the surface story. This level of fear can be divided into two types: Those that happen (aging, becoming disabled, dying, being alone, etc.) and those that require action (going back to school, changing careers, etc.)

The Second level is concerned with the ego: rejection, failure, being conned, success, etc. Level two fears concern the inner state of mind rather than exterior situations. This level reflects your ability to handle this world.

The Level Three Fear. At the bottom of every one of your fears is simply the fear that you can't handle whatever life may bring you.

Summary

Level 1: I can't handle illness, I can't handle losing him.

Level 2: I can't handle failure, I can't handle the responsibility of success.

Level 3: I can't handle it!

Solution to all fears:

If you knew you could handle anything that came your way, what would possibly have to fear? OR

I CAN HANDLE IT.

FIVE TRUTHS

TRUTH #1: The fear will never go away as long as I continue to grow.

TRUTH #2: The only way to get rid of the fear of doing something is to go out and do it.

TRUTH #3: The only way to feel better about myself is to go out.... and do it.

TRUTH #4: Not only am I going to experience fear whenever I'm on unfamiliar territory, but so is everyone else.

TRUTH #5: Pushing through fear is less frightening than living with the underlying fear that comes from a feeling of *helplessness.* Meaning: people who refuse to take risks live with a feeling of dread that is far more severe than what they would feel if they took the risks necessary to make them less helpless—only they don't know it.

Success Elements

Desire

Elements of success—desire

Every person who wins in any undertaking must be willing to burn his ships and cut all sources of retreat.

Six ways to turn desire into success (Gold)

1) Fix in your mind the exact amount of money you desire. (Output desired) or the exact goal/objective.

2) Determine exactly what you intend to give in return for the money you desire: Input

3) Establish a definite date when you intend to possess the money you desire.

4) Create a definite plan for carrying out your plan, and begin at once whether you are ready or not.

5) Write out a clear, concise statement of the plan with time frames, plan of action.

6) Review above plan every morning after waking up and before going to sleep. See and feel and believe yourself already in possession of the money.

7) There is a difference between wishing for a thing and being ready to receive it.

   a. No one is ready for a thing until he believes he can acquire it.

Thoughts Are Things

1) One (sound) idea is all that one needs to achieve success.

2) When you begin to *think* and grow rich, you will observe that riches begin with a state of mind, with *definiteness of purpose*, with little or no hard work.

3) We refuse to believe that which we do not understand.

Excusitis Causes Failure

Study people to discover characteristics of successful people.

Typical excuses: poor health, lack of education, too old/young, bad luck, wise, the way my family brought me up.

Don't be a wishful thinker. Don't waste your mental energies dreaming ways that are effortless to win success. Focus instead on those qualities that will make you a winner.

Brain Power and How to Boost It

Getting oxygen to the brain is essential in its function. Iron activates (turns on) the brain.

B Complex is essential to the brain.

B1 = Thiamine, B12 helps choline (memory enhancer).

Low B Complex level (B vitamins deficiency) leads to depression, abnormal behaviors, stress.

MAKING RELATIONSHIPS WORK

Isolating (identifying the problem)

The real problem must be pinpointed, otherwise the wrong solution will be found.

1) Method #1: Listen for themes behind your statements. Learn to recognize the themes that come up more frequently between you. Is it anger, money, sex, apathy, anxiety, lack of trust, lack of respect?

2) Method #2: To insure objectivity from being emotionally involved, write down your version of the problem. Be specific. Give evidence for each statement you make.

3) Start with a small problem and both learn the systematic way of arriving at a solution.

4) Establish rapport (open approach to each other) with each other.

5) Reduce hostility by:

6) Indirect release (inside a car insult spouse)

7) Ask why you are feeling so angry and find out—will reduce anger.

8) Reorient a person's attitude toward problem solving.

9) Positive homework assignments
   Make a written list of things you and your spouse have in common.
   a. Make a list of whatever your spouse does well.
   b. Role switching to see things from the other person's view.
   c. Record the fights and arguments and then listen to them when you're quiet to analyze problems.

No More Codependence

Codependency is a state of mind disease. A codependent person is one who has let another person's behavior affect him or her and who is obsessed with controlling that person's behavior. The heart of the definition and recovery lies not in the other person, it lies in ourselves.

Characteristics of a codependent:

1) Caretaking: warped responsibility, guilt, anger, victimized.

2) Low self worth: self-blame, defensive.

3) Repression: rigid, fear of self-expression.

4) Obsession: worry, unable to stop talking about people.

5) Controlling

6) Denial—lie to oneself

7) Dependency

8) Poor communication

9) Weak boundaries—threaten and not act.

10) Lack of trust—trust unworthy people

11) Anger—feel scared, hurt, and angry

12) Sex problems

13) Miscellaneous: be extremely responsible or irresponsible

SELF CARE

1) Detachment—is releasing or detaching from a person or problem in love: mentally, emotionally, and sometimes physically—disengage ourselves from unhealthy entanglements with another person's life, and from problems we cannot solve.

2) How to detach—as best as we can. How = honesty and openness and willingness to try.

3) Not be a reactionary

Keep oneself in a crisis state: tense, high flow of adrenaline.

You are not responsible for making other people see the light and you do not need to "set them straight". You are responsible for helping yourself see the light and for setting yourself straight.

"God, grant me the serenity to accept the things I cannot change, the courage to change the things I can, and the wisdom to know the difference." The Serenity Prayer.

Three things humans can do

1) Thinking
2) Feeling: Emotions, feelings: irritated, amused, happy, guilty, furious, intense, depressed
3) Behaving (acting)

FATAL MISTAKES

1) Excessive anxiety—nervous, tense, upset, agitated, intimidated, afraid, freaked out, scared. When in this state of mind you cannot handle situations effectively.

2) Angry (defensive, furious, outraged, ticked off, frustrated). In this state of mind also you cannot work properly.

3) Depressed or burned out—bummed out, don't give a damn, ignoring, uncaring, also not an effective behavior.

4) Excessively making self guilty—overly responsible, remorseful, blameful, and you will make decisions for all the wrong reasons (because I feel guilty).

THE ABCs OF BUTTON PUSHING

A's are the pushers. In order to keep people from pushing your buttons, you start by figuring out what/who really causes your reactions in the first place.

There are two activating events

1) Major crises (floods, hurricanes, diseases). We usually handle these biggies properly.

2) Daily activities—hassles, frustrations, worries, problems, decisions, and difficult people whom we let bother us and push our buttons.

C's represent two things: your feelings and behavior in the specific situation occurring at point A. For example, getting stuck in a traffic jam causes anger, agitation.

A   Activating event: specific situation or people.

B   Your beliefs about activating events (your perception).

C   Your feelings and behavior (your response).

B's: What we do at point B where we run into difficult situations or persons at Point A *before* we wind up feeling or acting at point C.

At Point B we do many things: react, chose, perceive, decide, analyze, make judgement, assess, imagine.... all summed up in: WE THINK. Therefore the way we think in response to a specific person or situation will largely determine both our response (emotionally and behaviorally) at C, and whether we let A push our buttons, or not.

Therefore, A's don't cause C's. B's cause C's (They just don't think at all, they just REACT.)

Test plan—instead of avoiding people and situations that push your buttons, deliberately approach these situations and desensitize yourself to button pushers.

Nutty beliefs we use to let others push our buttons: To control our reactions we must understand how we upset ourselves, how to change our overreactions.

At point B we have 3 beliefs:

1) Catastrophic thinking—we make things bigger than they are. (What if....) causes many catastrophic thoughts: What if he does not love me anymore? Solution: Figure the worst outcome of "what if..." and accept it.

2) Absolutist thinking: I must, I should, I've got to, I need to, I have to, I ought to, etc. Parents, TV, teachers instill these habits.

3) Rationalization (underreactions): they are poor attempts to deny or play down what is happening. We try to make sense of or to justify our questionable behavior.

4) Realistic preferences are hard to implement but very possible: I want, I'd like, I prefer....

Ten (10) Bad Push Buttons

a. Worrying too much about what others think of us. Excessive worrying creates a strong fear or rejection.

b. Fear of failure: If I fail it's terrible and I cannot stand it.

c. Low frustration tolerance—people and things should always turn out the way I want them to—and if they don't it is horrible and I can't stand it.

d. Blame others: if I'm not respected, if I fail, or if things don't go my way I'll always blame someone else for it.

e. If I worry obsessively about some event things will turn out better.

f. Perfect solutions exist for every problem and I must find them—no such thing.

g. It is easier to avoid difficult situations and responsibilities than to face them.

h. If I never get seriously involved in anything, and maintain a detached perspective, I will never be unhappy.

i. My past (childhood, love relationship, job) is what is causing me to feel and act this way now.

j. Bad people and things should not exist and they are the cause of my disturbance.

Change your irrational thinking. This requires: commitment, awareness, practice.

Awareness—what I am thinking to myself about myself, about the others in the situation, and about the situation.

Couples as Button Pushers

1) Couples always assume some expectations from each other. He/she will be/change and that is OK.

2) Measure of a relationship's success: the ability to resolve differences, conflicts, problems, differences in opinion/values/ wants/preferences/priorities is the critical factor.

Five factors for a good relationship:

1) Communication: ability to discuss (as opposed to fight, debate, argue) to solve the problem at hand.

2) Sense of humor

3) Commitment: no other relationship is more important

4) Flexibility: being able to admit one's mistakes and change position or view.

5) Love and respect each other.

After you try 1) Discussing and fail 2) try counseling and still failing, 3) go and separate.

BUILDING SELF-CONFIDENCE STRATEGIES

1) Practice: practice makes a skill a habit. Practice—skill—habit

2) Behave "as if": As if you are confident and you will be. Adopt confidence in your posture and action and thoughts and you will get it.

3) Take the zigzag path: be flexible not rigid in pursuing your goals.

4) Make the most of your mistakes and then ignore them. Making mistakes is a part of living, but one must recognize the mistake and use it to get back on track. If you fail try again. Mistakes are a source of information.

5) Be kind to yourself. Problems with self-esteem (confidence) are rooted sometimes in a bad habit of punishing ourselves and not rewarding ourselves properly. Treat yourself with kindness and respect.

6) Limit self-blame. Kicking yourself for past mistakes or failures makes you waver. Replace self-blame with encouraging voices.

HOW TO BREAK YOUR ADDICTION TO A PERSON

1) Attachment hunger- the basis of addiction.

2) Symptoms of addiction to a person

3) Compulsive quality

4) The panic one feels at the possible absence of the substance (the thought of breaking the relationship)

5) Withdrawal

6) After the mourning period triumph, sense of liberation, and accomplishment is realized.

Are you addicted? Symptoms

1) Even though your objective judgements (and others) tell you that your relationship is BAD for you, you take no effective steps to break it.

2) You give yourself reasons for staying in it that do not hold water.

3) When you think about ending the relationship you feel dread, terror, and you cling to it even harder.

4) When you take steps to end it, you suffer acute withdrawal symptoms, including physical distress.

5) When the relationship is really over (or you fantasize that it has ended), you feel lostness, aloneness.

When you are in an addictive relationship, it is essential that you understand the roots of your addiction.

Levels of Linkage

1) The Practical Considerations: When children are involved and financial dependence and long-standing relationship.

2) Belief: beliefs you hold about relationships in general, about specific troubled relationships and about yourself. Example: "Love is forever", 'love conquers all", "the most important thing is security", all of these beliefs force one to make the wrong decisions.

3) Hunger Attachment: everyone starts as an infant. Feelings of the attachment hunger level make a person an addict only if these feelings are so strong that they can override his ability to act in his own best interest. Attachment hunger is the fuel of your addiction. To free yourself of its power, you must learn all you can about it and how it operates in your life.

The Return of a Memory

In order to understand your attachment hunger, it is essential that you realize that it is not a new experience. It is not occurring (again) for the first time in the current relationship. It is the return of a memory. It is an emotional reminiscence of a much earlier time. This means when you are ruled by attachment hunger, your mind is re-experiencing the state you were in as an infant or toddler.

How can you keep yourself from being dominated by these intense physiological responses?

For one thing, you must stop fooling yourself with those cliched beliefs.

The bodily reactions of attachment hunger simply come from a level other than your judgement, a level so early in your history that it is hardly a guide to what you, as an adult, should do.

I cannot live without you.

If you become dependent on a particular person to make you feel you exist, then you are paying a high emotional price even when the relationship is at its best.

To break a relationship one must (sooner or later) risk facing the terror.

Identity: you are your daddy's son. Son has no identity without daddy. Ideally, it would be nice if by this time in your life your sense of your identity was clear and firm. If you must get your affirmation from the reflected approval of others, and most of us do, it is far better to get it from many people than to be dependent only on one person—because one person might have only distorted views.

You are my security blanket

If you are deriving your feelings of security or worth from a relationship that is making you unhappy, then it will be helpful for you to explore the origins of your underlying feelings of insecurity or poor self-esteem.

Peaks and Valleys

In helping yourself to cope with the extremeness of emotions involved in breaking an addiction, if you do not feel ready for a full cold—turkey withdrawal, you might consider temporary separation and allow yourself to experience the feelings of being without the person.

The object of my affection

(Why we select always the same mate-type)—self-esteem has a lot to do with it and childhood.

Self-delusion and Addiction

To keep yourself hanging in there you may have learned how to fool yourself into believing you are happy, to anesthetize the pain, to gloss over the disappointment. It is understandable that we would want to delude ourselves about unpleasant realities when our attachment hunger pushes us to stay there, but that is as dangerous as taking pain killers to block out the side effects of illness.

Self Deceptive Maneuvers

1) Rationalization: send sense for senseless cases.
2) Idealization: when he/she is your attachment hunger fetish, you distort who she is in a way that plays up her deeds and actions and diminishes her bad points. Almost any trait or characteristic can be idealized for the purpose of self-delusion.

Unfounded Hope

Look coldly at the facts not the wishful thinking. Do not distort your objectives.

The Art of Staying Hooked

The methods used to control a relationship so the attachment hunger goal is achieved are five methods:

1) Control through power: macho male or bitchy female ("do it my way or else") or "I will leave you". Old adage: Do not make yourself so big, you're not so small.

Your partner is trying to have the upper hand. Domineering partner: you might respond by submission, which leads you to: suffocation, depression, anger, outrage. You conclude that the only way possible is to leave.

Alternative solution: you refuse to submit to unreasonable domination. Stop battling for supremacy. Example: Just because I don't do what you want does mean I don't love you. Ask yourself: Am I staying only because I am scared, or does my fear mask my attachment hungry infant's reluctance to break this tie?

2) Controlling through weakness:
    Manifesto: I am weak, helpless, dependent, and will fall apart without you. Remember your partner is not that fragile.

3) Control through servitude:
    My case: He came to understand how his self-doubts arose in his relationship with his parents who were hard working, dedicated, but emotionally constricted people. Getting emotional response from them was difficult, but he learned early that they valued hard work and service and that he could feel loved and accepted by being helpful.
    If servitude is your game, ask yourself: I will make myself useful, so indispensable that you will be bound to me and you will be unable to leave me.

4) Control through guilt: Do what I want. Do not do what I want and I will not love you. Stop shouting at me, I am getting those headaches again.

5) Vulnerability to jealousy: based on 2 fears. 1) Fear of losing the other partner. 2) The fear that if our partner becomes involved with someone else, it means that we are no good (not true).

The vulnerability place makes it possible for your partner to provoke jealousy in you in order to intensify your involvement with him and as a way of getting you to value him more highly, because the arousal of jealousy accomplishes both these things (high intensity and involvement).

His vulnerability to jealousy allows you to arouse jealousy in him as a way to intensify his involvement with you and value you more.

Stimulating jealousy can be a dangerous power manipulation in love relationships. It is dangerous because it arouses feelings that are opposite to those that make for a good relationship.

Instead of trust there is distrust.

Instead of tenderness there is rage.

Instead of friendliness there is vindictiveness.

Instead of serenity there is turmoil.

But should I end it?

Use relationship satisfaction Cost/Benefit analysis. Rate as 1 = very high, 2 = high, 3 = fair, 4 = low,

5 = very low.

1) General emotional contentment

2) Communication

3) Companionship

4) Sharing of interests

5) Practical support

6) Emotional support

7) Growth support

8) Feeling loved by my partner

9) Feeling love toward by partner

10) Feeling respected by my partner

11) Feeling respect for my partner

12) Feeling trusted by my partner

13) Feeling trusting of my partner

14) Feeling nurtured by my partner

15) Feeling nurturing toward my partner

16) Enjoyment
17) Warmth
18) Sexual satisfaction
19) Feeling of self-esteem
20) Desire to spend time with my partner

RISKS

1) If your life is ever going to get better, you will have to take risks.

2) To risk is to exceed one's usual limits in reaching goals, and to accept as real uncertainty and danger as part of the process.

3) Everything you really want in life avoids taking a risk.

4) In every risk is some unavoidable loss, something that has to be given to move ahead.

5) People fear being rejected, but unless a person risks being rejected, never finds a love he can trust.

6) Not risking is the surest way of losing.

7) There is a point when you lose more by waiting than by doing.

8) He sees his duty as all -consuming because he is afraid to look at his life as a free person. He holds himself responsible for others before himself and this keeps him from taking actions for his own good (responsible first for self). Accept responsibility to act in your own best interests.

How do you know that you wouldn't be better off staying the way you are?

1) Admit to yourself that:
   a. You are not where you want to be.
   b. You are not feeling the way you think you should.
   c. You are not happy.
      i. To maintain the old self-deception once you become aware makes your life less real and drains your energy.

ii. An investment of friendship—like any bad money invest-ment—or love is no less painful to lose than of one of money.

iii. Attachments held out of fear do not really serve us.

iv. You are supposed to be afraid when you risk.

v. The truth is that success falls to the courageous person rather than to those who understand and plan everything but cannot act.

vi. You can never be helpful to others until you can help your-self first.

vii. The truth is that no one can ever fulfill you except you.

viii. The adolescent comes of age when he can accept his faults and still believe he is good.

ix. You would not be where you are now unless you had taken risks, and will not be where you want to be without risking more.

x. Each person fears three general kinds of loss in life: loss of love, control, and esteem. Our childhood responses to above losses shape our personality and how we deal with these losses.

xi. It is only with that complete acceptance of yourself (no fear of rejection) that you will become independent of others' opinions of your worth.

xii. Control: when a person fears losing control, any possible weakness appears as a serious threat, and energy consuming, and taking any risk causes great anxiety.

xiii. What you can control: money and property and things. You cannot control: feelings and people. Feelings need to be expressed.

The Moment of Risk

Risking is broken down into three phases: 1) Preparation 2) Commitment 3) Completion

Phase 1: Preparation

Step 1: Your need to risk if you are in danger. Admitting in a relationship, for example, that one must do something (take a risk to change status quo) leads to questions. Do what, when, how?

One must admit to the problem and define it and move swiftly to solve it.

Step 2: Deciding to risk: We all know someone who admitted that he is dissatisfied in general in life, in love, or career, yet still can't seem to decide anything about the situation.

1) The fear of exposure: do you fear failure and being labeled as a failure?

2) You can't make a good decision if you do not understand why you fear making it.

3) Keeping perspective: It is important to make a plan for taking the risk and following through it as well as an alternative plan (Plan B) in case of failure (failure of plan A).

4) Getting your bearings: Make alternative solution B (Plan B).

Phase 2: Committing

Step 3: Committing to pass—starting the risk. This is the action step. When a spouse talks of separation, the other party cries and causes scenes and guilt. Be strong with resolve.

Step 4: The point of no return: you might feel cold feet at this stage. When a person reaches the no return stage he must gather momentum and power and reassert his convictions in his goal. This stored power consists of accepting goals and coming to terms to move on. Do not let any doubt or anyone instill doubt in what you are doing. Underlying fears: in risks of love people fear: being rejected, hurt, hurtful, losing love for themselves, etc.

In risks of power, people fear losing whatever they used to control (being weak, bad, angry, impotent, unfit, cruel, or vulnerable).

In risks of esteem, people fear losing face, reputation, they dread being embarrassed, made fun of, ridiculed, fear of their feelings made public, if they did not accept their feelings already.

Phase 3: Completing the Risk

Step 5: Leaving the old: For dependent people, the difficulty of risking is in leaving the familiar behind. It may be: the old home, job, old friends and lovers suddenly begin to take on a soft, idealistic glow when they are abandoned, making them seem better than they were.

People who risk for love often feel ambivalent about fulfilling themselves, especially when they hurt others.

Adapting: the best plan is one that is always adapting, where everyone expects to change.

EMOTIONAL RISKS

The most important risk you can take is to be honest in expressing your feelings. If you do not express what you feel, you are forced to use defenses to keep unwanted feelings away.

A defense is built into your character. Defenses rob you of your energy and transform you into a person who does only what he thinks is acceptable (conform) because he feels uncomfortable being himself.

1) When a loss threatens, you feel anxious.

2) When a loss occurs, you feel hurt.

3) When hurt is held back, it becomes anger.

4) When anger is held back, it creates guilt.

5) When guilt is unrelieved, depression occurs.

6) If you take care of your fear, hurt, and anger, the guilt and depression will take care of themselves.

7) Fear is the threat of loss or an injury. It may be a real loss or just imaginary.

8) Knowing what you are afraid of will make your fear easier to manage.

9) To take risks successfully, you must become aware of and familiar with your own experience of fear. Just like a driver speeding, speeding causes threat of injury (fear) but if a driver anticipated that, then he would have managed properly. Separation causes threat of loss and love—being aware can make separation easy and doable.

10) Coping with fear: imagine the worst outcome and accept it, then try to improve on it.

To Risk Admitting Hurt

Real strength is being able to admit one's weakness honestly, to say that one is hurt and afraid, and still take a forceful stand and carry on. Real strength comes from accepting your vulnerability.

To Risk Expressing Anger

1) Expressing anger—to tell the person who hurt you that he did so. Do it simply and directly and state that you feel angry. Then wait for his response.

2) If a person does not love you because you get angry when he hurts you, he did not love you before.

3) If you are afraid of losing control by getting angry and therefore hold it in, you are only setting yourself up for the day when you cannot hold it in anymore.

4) What is a relationship worth in which you cannot express yourself (what you feel)?

5) You have to risk being true to your feelings or you can never be true to yourself.

6) Anger is the natural result of being hurt, injured, let down, disappointed, tricked, made a fool of, taken advantage of, used, insulted, ridiculed.

7) If you hold anger in all the time, it can destroy you.

NEURO   ASSOCIATIVE CONDITIONING (NAC)

NAC Master Step 1: Decide what you really want and what is preventing you from having it.

If we focus on what we do not want, we will get more out of it, therefore we must concentrate on what we really want.

Mostly we link pain to changing when we must link pleasure to what we want.

NAC Master step 2: get leverage. Associate massive pain to not changing now and massive pleasure to changing now. The only way we're going to change now is by creating a sense of urgency that is so intense to get changing now. Fear no change, have no mixed emotions. Associate massive pain to not changing and massive pleasure to changing now. [Change = pleasure].

NAC Master Step 3: Interrupt the limiting pattern. The challenge is that most people want a new result, but continue to act in the same way. Knowing what you want and your leverage and having motivation, but keeping doing the same things will keep us in pain and results in zero change. Think of some ways you can interrupt your own patters (frustration, worry, overwhelm). A simple way of breaking a pattern is by scrambling the sensations we link to our memories.

Practice: Think of a situation that makes you feel sad, frustrated, or angry.

Master Step 4: Create a new, empowering alternative: If old pattern is not replaced change stops here (no success.). In any case, I will have freedom from headaches, fighting and all the pains. I will have a new life free to pain and full of joy and good challenges. [Empowering change—happy life.]

Master Step 5: Condition the new pattern until it's consistent. If you rehearse the new empowering alternative continually with massive emotional intensity, it will become a habit for new results. Remember, your brain cannot differentiate between what you imagine and what you experience.

Set a schedule to reinforce your new behavior: reward yourself immediately whenever you succeed in acquiring new behavior (not worrying and taking action entitles you to a reward). Your nervous system links in this way great pleasures to change.

Mark Twain said "there is nothing training cannot do. Nothing is above its reach. It can turn bad morals to good, it can destroy bad principles and recreate good ones, I can lift men to angelship."

Note that reinforcement is responding to a behavior immediately after it occurs, while punishment and reward may occur long afterward.

NAC Master Step 6:—Test it!

Summary: You've decided upon the new pattern of emotion or behavior that you desire, you've gotten leverage on yourself to change it, you've interrupted the old pattern, you've found a new alternative, and you've conditioned it until it's consistent. The only step left is to test it and make sure it will work in the future.

Summary

1) Define desired new pattern of behavior or emotion.
2) Get leverage to change yourself.
3) Interrupt the old pattern.
4) Find an alternative.
5) Do consistent conditioning.
6) Test.

7) Decide what you really want and what's preventing you from having it now.

8) Get leverage: associate massive pain to not changing now and massive pleasure to changing now.

9) Interrupt the limiting pattern by scrambling the sensations we link to our memories. 1—See the situation in your mind that was bothering you, picture it as a movie—don't feel angry, just watch it. 2—Turn that situation into a funny cartoon, run it backward very fast and forward with music and with funny Pinocchio nose and Mickey Mouse look. This will break the old associated pattern and produce a new one, just like being interrupted.

10) Create a new, empowering alternative. If alternative not found, just find a model who did it. Example: it takes a woman to forget one.

11) Condition the new pattern until it's consistent. Use reinforcement to condition your pattern.

12) Test the pattern to see if it works.

REGAINING SELF-ESTEEM IS A SKILL

Some people think that self-esteem / confidence, courage, and other human characteristics are born with us. In other words, some people had them from birth. The fact of the matter is that all human characteristics are learned after birth. Self-esteem is a major part of any human being, he or she learns as he/she grows. This process of learning, by definition, makes self-esteem a skill that can be learned and developed. This is good news for all of us, even for the completely stripped of self-esteem or the one of us with a low self-esteem because we can develop our self-esteem like we develop any skill.

Developing or regaining self-esteem basically requires us to systematically follow some simple steps. The first step is very essential; believe that you are as good as the next person, that you are an *EQUAL* equipped with ALL THE TOOLS everybody else has; a brain, a body, a spirit, and the whole nine yards. Like my brother used to say, "when all men undress, they all look alike". He also used to say "all people go to the bathroom and perform the same things, piss and discharge". I find this simplistic view and humorous depiction of man very true, obviously, and most importantly it lays the foundation for building one's self-esteem. For it is true that all people are built the same way and have the same physical and mental building blocks.

What distinguishes one from another is how one develops himself and since self-esteem is a skill, therefore anyone can develop his/her self-esteem. Reading this book a few times will help you develop your self-esteem. One reading is not enough.

ABOUT THE AUTHOR

When I told my friends I am writing a book about self-esteem, I was pleased to hear all of them say, "that is a good topic because you are good with people and you know how to help them". Psychology and self-help books started to interest me more that 30 years ago. As a child I read every book I could find in the library and then summarized it. I read thousands of self-help and general psychology books in French, Arabic, and English. Human behavior fascinates and intrigues me. Its study became a mission for me. Can studying human behavior as it relates to its causes, manifestations and its roots be framed logically and can we trace the roots causing an abnormal/normal behavior? Is human behavior an acquired skill and if so can we change our life to make it happy and successful?

After decades of real life experience and theoretical research studying, I came to the conclusion that indeed our logical mind and our behavior are interrelated and behavior affects our mind and vice-versa. My experience in life taught me that action indeed can influence our minds, moods, feelings, and all our psyche (Regain your Self-Esteem).

I wrote RYSE to show that our happiness, success, health (mental and physical), and in a word our well-being can be influenced positively or negatively. We can control the quality of our self-esteem by controlling the thoughts, and the components that build our self-esteem: our entire past, and our present. My divorce prompted me to write RYSE as a guide for me and people who have been subjected to childhood abuse, put downs, and spousal systematic self-esteem destruction. However, self-esteem can be regained by reversing the pattern that caused it in the first place.

In RYSE I am offering my readers life tested methods, and ideas that will make them successful and happy.

www.ingramcontent.com/pod-product-compliance
Lightning Source LLC
Chambersburg PA
CBHW031241280526
45784CB00004B/1662